D1125197

MONKEYS,
MINOR PLANET,
AVERAGE STAR

MONKEYS, MINOR PLANET, AVERAGE STAR

GRACIE LEAVITT

NIGHTBOAT BOOKS

BROOKLYN & CALLICOON, NEW YORK

THE HAWK VISIT

FROM A GRAFTED TREE

Jean-Luc Godard: *I think it was Truffaut who said—and the same thing goes for my films—that in his films there was 20 percent autobiography, 20 percent things you've read, 20 percent things you've heard, or been told, 20 percent fiction, and 20 percent something else I don't remember.*

Philippe Labro: *And what are you shooting tomorrow?*

Godard: *We're filming a scene in the subway, where it goes up above ground.*

GAP GARDENING I

Thin cover

Having wryly put conditions
on of love what can be said
for this that Irma rolls my head
from scalar milkweed rods
oblique to down-slope creep
and young snow patch, one pale
finch sips our slue just past
two half inch male pipe threads,
thin hose, spring loaded preset valve
control, inchoate on square lawn
unmowed, dust unsuppressed,
some scumbled mess no spigot
oscillates about these narrow
brumal shallows tapered under
his catalpa, ornamental, painted
white, silk cabled off from cinder
path we dart cross lots unseen
to make the going predicate.
Have said the same before if you
recall, that we might down-slip
in tin washtub Irma squats
in Helen's skirts beside if only
now not calved and hipped
too big for this to fail,
even overturning all.

Riparian ephemera in October for spring

I.   A rush of ink in the tall grasses—his heft of marginalia in my hands.

II. His hand in her hair on his knee by the bed; her hands in the grass later on—how quick the soup came off.

III. She was a honey with a hand, a balloon on a string, on a day milt mixed with her roe in the weed, vanishing.

IV. Never to have picked apart the rock, to have sunk the thumb in marrow deep—in alb, in milky mud—as she rowed by.

V.   At first blush the fetid crab apples were his in my hands—later crushed upon the walk, later held up to our radiator as it bled.

Paradox of heap, circa 1938

Gawky, limp, akimbo, dawdles
aft rough gray-blue sky of anvil
clouds accreting, pale cicadas
divide odd air, in bottle-green
coat, the worse for wear, one girl
on a railway station platform
somewhere middling– No? Is all
that's left of misery back then?
Such as it is... Fiddles with...
Kicks leaves and scrap and dust
clots drain ditch curved below,
ago she curved in, settled little
primrose-tinted night a milky
film upon his face who mawkish
laughs beside her, dear but not
quite near to him in measure, he
she so well loved once dangled
off coal pier, boards of which
since have buckled, splintered,
fallen in.

Morton's Fork

Unweaves, she, midscene, pockmarked,
the path through deepwood lily from
men digging at gray dayfall at its margins
where our border ponies are who suck
on pulp I offer up, wet threads got out
of hand, as did those autumn-sullen Rites
of Coy Amanuensis on his four poster
last night when she failed one rabbit
test then threw a tantrum in the zone
where I belong or would by his initial
parallax. From here our branch line offers
little but your face in their spit-shine:
jejune and contrapuntal to the whole
of what's gone on. As every rabbit dies.

Egdon Heath

One coat lay kneaded by moon best felt when not clearly seen, in summer days subdued, oversad, stretched hollow and exhaling. Her wild briary shoulders embrowned, the furzy sparse, a spot of dawn rolled overhead on distant rims overlaid—dividing time, no less. Who can say of a particular sea that is old, shutting out sky...? When was young was its lover—a spot on whitish road, rolling, branched, against this pallid screen; it had a lonely face, as with some long lived apart passed unheeded as, awaiting one dark proof to be aroused. Thorough-going in the myrtle garden, inviolate in very white raiment, we await and shake opaque one last spot of dawn. It had a lonely face, it reclined upon a stump, brooding to sleep—oftener not thought of after dreaming till revived by scenes like this.

To comprehend this total scheme we note that long ago a man went though [sic] the woods, as you may have done, and I certainly have, trying to find the shortest way through the woods in a given direction. He found trees fallen across his path. He climbed over those crisscrossed trees and suddenly found himself poised on a tree that was slowly teetering. It happened to be lying across another great tree, and the other end of the tree on which he found himself teetering lay under a third great fallen tree. As he teetered he saw the third big tree lifting. It seemed impossible to him. He went over and tried using his own muscles to lift that great tree. He couldn't budge it. Then he climbed back atop the first smaller tree, purposefully teetering it, and surely enough it again elevated the larger tree. I'm certain that the man who found such a tree thought that it was a magic tree, and may have dragged it home and erected it as man's first totem. It was probably a long time before he learned that any stout tree would do, and thus extracted the concept of the generalized principle of leverage out of all his earlier successive special-case experiences with such accidental discoveries.

—R. Buckminster Fuller

On the axis but across from each magnolia

Mirror-black birds stiff
on mirror-black boughs,
it's mudtime, edenic,
vogue pampa under stars
or depending where you are
a drumlin, pitchblende, grayed,
of rose hip, chicken scratch
we chat long into night
beer-sour from mock sun
unmitigated, actions in
the shade we'll never—
all our arms, our legs stuck out
from blossoms tossed from
trees in tongues and clots
and threes, pink-tipped,
chatoyant, cluttering ghat
we wobble down where you
whose lover is banal watch
while I wade in these I pass
weld to then peel from me as if
I'd found the spot all roads
you'd meant to find convened.
But pond skin thin as drum paper
breaks in the end with just
one beat too hard: She dives;
you turn; I see your face
as would I on your final thrust.

Recombinant plasma of the pre-dawn star at neap tide

Was out back by those hay swaths where
he moored her to the terebinth we climbed
or were recumbent in ago she imagined
as drupes dropping clingstones just below
one foreshore bobwhite heap of mother's
maidhood damp with algae of the cove since
she could no longer sleep stood up in chasmal
soft leaf mold, knee-deep– In air so green
with mayflies, his breath rank with crop milk,
say this only once, I'll be your daughter
only, fool, who was a boy on some local
empty beach from where she was mere
glimpse, simply, askance, bold in a bay
window backlit. To put a sharper point
on it I did and still grip spider mums.

Deballasted

Jupes rouges et bleues et brunes forsook
or sloppy cast off, rather, in some patch
of molted shade tainted alternate of sun,
meantime he, doltish, sick on the carpet,
sulks, his bailing can of hedge apple
upturned in our fount, they motile,
bobbing off. Unstoppers dark paps
to his lips, apatetic in the toft, sings:
"Here I am again in Bolivia, dreaming,
oh, the tangerines you'll open, every
one, and then not feed me one of!"
Now he knows it all as only from
a hilltop wholly made of scree much
attended by old men tidal several
miles above their mouths, he sobs
silently, winded, and the ard takes off
the first of dirt as often as not, as any
other thing, as in cassocks on his porch
others, lofty, ply contrarily unawares,
etiolate, beseated, some in waiting, some
in wanting, querulous, lumpen. All's
as often as not, as any other thing,
two ptyxis shows, waging love, volute,
before him form from under ard
and infinite. Anyway, who was it there
cast off their skirts, all hues? Say,
just when will they come back?

Paradox of heap, circa 1929

Was once one weakly brook turned creek
by which we kneel since could not ford
within dense boxwood hid as they did from
Malvolio, daft, as dunnage drifts to shore,
to daylong jaw of her, your kisscurl love,
a cutpurse strung all tissue skirt, off-white,
gloam come through, cleft, wind-clung,
tunes curb to shrub we ease apart or reach
among, and clumsy tickle trout, together
rubbed and gripped, wet upon peignoir
rumpled with noon-dull on which its vitals
spill, in which you'll later gentle fold her
meal, that yonder moll, your kisscurl love.

Backwards compatible

They pad your tow road down clear to
that riven pine bough weir from where
we abseil toward caught cowslip taut
in sluice gates stuck half shut as precondition
to his down-slope sawmill pond full
stanchioned off with red cords strung
between for keeping black swan problems
out, this log pond left unsucked; he stroke
delimbs, she plunges in, has gotten all
her gingham wet, so dries along your weir
though one hem snags a pin and slams
those sluice gates shut. Some like poles
in the field, I guess, for we who won't
have won if you don't want us.

If you are in a shipwreck and all the boats are gone, a piano top buoyant enough to keep you afloat that comes along makes a fortuitous life preserver. But this is not to say that the best way to design a life preserver is in the form of a piano top. I think that we are clinging to a great many piano tops in accepting yesterday's fortuitous contrivings as constituting the only means for solving a given problem.

–R. Buckminster Fuller

Reverse the charm that crushes she

for Emma Bee Bernstein, who took beautiful pictures (1985-2008)

They are oars in quiet water in motion with her leading us who caterwaul, who loll among the awkward hawks in winter's cowl on Herring Cove, warm; but daydreams concussed; but ours hitched to hers; but the wind drowned out my question of you I know not of, she, so milk-white, implacable, both Giotto angel and Jezebel, both little breasts and big eyes, who haunted every aperture, even pulling outrageous stockings on, plus dancing in and out about the bonfire on Grand and smoked a cigarette, was swept away, letting her drink to itself, sweating there, misfigured, about the fire. So when come upon where they have called and day-dark is in Venice and is labyrinthine, is doing this in vain, we watch the brighter waves but idle ruled in light we wake, us two, and take from summer woods, like sleek linnet, rippling. In faith, we did for all we could, still they found you on the floor; next day The Peggy Guggenheim was closed; canals seemed out of phase with them who rowed them. Later we lie down in green pasture, quiet water; later you lay a table out before me and fill my cup; it spills—the oil—your eyes—I'll never have your eyes—reflect this quiet water, uncanny in the cup; misfigures a soul lolling with hawks in chaos and abrupt. Now come close, as the vine comes close, and passions part too strange, to share the last of it, of course, with me you know not of, the last to hear this news, I guess. Ms. Midnight, come stumbling to surround in a pattern held not so well so long, showed cold apple blossom in her hair to her and called her by another name and finished out her joy with him and moaned, as all do who are young in colored robes, in the folds and faded of— Would we have pecked your nowhere hands, milk-white, should we have known you then; would we have shown you shade of some oak not to break on leaning in that magic hour you so well loved so long before laying down your head in that same hour, not so dumbfounded as we who go on rowing.

15

...look / through that window only slightly / mutter verbs like persuade, probe, / phrenology, fellow, transgress against / that diaphragmatic urge to be again / "that girl" time marked by shoe sizes, / length of hair...   —Erica Kaufman

...First, I was a concept... / No, I was a little girl.
Who knows the difference?   —Alice Notley

FIFTH-GRADE OPHELIA

The Young-Girl is not always young; more and more frequently, she is not even female. She is the figure of total integration in a disintegrating social totality.
—Tiqqun, translated by Ariana Reines

It is never a good thing to speak against a little girl.   —Roland Barthes

1

Then I was a fifth-grade Ophelia, tall order, was that biplane dream you did
not have of her emended in a public place or paratexted to yourself, virga
was the scrim, double scrim, not a soda in my hand, stuck with what I have,
I can go on in ways above the unprimed field calcined or strip mall arterial
or disused gasworks site when is effaced that genitive beast swage terminates
to disappoint our objectscape strategically, dovetail this landslip and outcrop
booleanly, were outward facing then, she irresisting under preassembled hedge
of furze we haptic navigate, patchily divided, apt, under syzygy half-overcast,
under his substantial fascinator's weight lounged selling reported speech
or actionable scenes in celluloid by fiat for sleeping car porter brothers withal,
the lottery, the taxi dance, stone stiles you leaned against, how it was, as if
some small turf fire or conceit at veritable quay sheds primal yellow coat
provisionally to moan at littoral zone of untrammeled love-play off-base
dismantled of names the skittish novice names as would you in short susurrate
bland fuck noise out, not a soda in her hand, she lingers, pivots, I do, he won't,
how it is to need not your oven bird nor diminish any thing nor cease and be another.

#2

Then I was a fifth-grade Ophelia, unsorted, she status post diagnosed plus three
months coital exposure, was this individual rendered through the general and vice
versa, cyanotically, perhaps, unlikely, thanks to cul-de-sac adhesions, thick, recurring,
but full-term, thanks to Danazol injections daily your father gave your mother
in the ass, thanks to blow-by, half expecting worse, yet like a lure in water came,
loose Joycean close third, as rerun theater of my consideration informs, as if
on an open court essentially one air-conditioned eve, glitterized, reglitterized,
incalculably he cadent strode inductile like your lure in water then I'm conjugated
half expecting worse or equal threat postponed at viaduct, not some place else,
off at the pass, a lot of years, diaphoretic, non-med compliant, "waltzing in
sweet chewing gum haze, knees slightly crooked," Henry said, cool as a geranium,
faunal after fucking, cyan of interstitial program glowing midst—blessing everything,
blessing the furniture, fiscally beside itself in lower flower district, violaceous,
swoons, such narrowing of its arm above the elbow, waviform, its blouse blown off
some rock or through your window, dismal end-user, excepting lodged-there AC unit,
tight fit. My outcrop, eloquent area, of stopless downburst damage, saplings torn,
plays poor incidental host to love among the artists, he said, makes me one, yet
who's gone through the windshield since, who's to say, who's suffered barotrauma
in her jumping bath and complementary goods. Wonder these days who's to say
what we two say to each other—iff filed away, iff booleanly. "You have a sister
more beautiful than yourself, you say. Show her to me—" Pretty follow-on product
of Danazol injection, of faunal succession, hurt in the soil mantle, not cool
as a geranium, born blue the way the sky is blue, refracted, vasoconstricted.

#3

Then I was a fifth-grade Ophelia, was hedging your bets, off course,
strong-stressed, every way which is natural when what a cool little figure
slips you turn her tiny tits just as he does, complete, but tell me next about
yourself remotely like what this implies in carbon offset site, my precious
practico-inert, is in wet calico nightshirt, every way is natural, dumb,
lowbrow, is kindred gardening in heels, in pantomime, can't possibly graph,
in the end, range of suitable habitat, glued by his head to a rock, if you
should pry him from this rock, consider inheritability, consider suicidality,
little elbowroom, not cut out for every way out of—left to its own devices
happens more than we think. See in distal nettle bower lacewings' efficacious
flexure of, or here above knocked down drop ceiling panels which conceal
lacewing-occluded vents no older than aunts' use of them. Not for nothing
is where my head is at. Is summarized as your want which not at all
you want if not at once to live wherever it looks like that, still able to walk
his horses out it all washed up facsimile. Lyn's "been a blind camera all day
in preparation for this dream." Paul says "a flower, a proposition, a noise
can be imagined almost simultaneously..." This stuff crops up all over the place.
Will share my parts with you, will give you all my parts, wonders keep
our stars apart, discrete, in the end, aboutness obscures that god-term
as you called it then, appointed passably in these parts in such amounts
as lacewing, noise, as nettle bower in the way of fecund autumn's air supply.

#4

Then I was a fifth-grade Ophelia, deboarded, were our formal gestures baggage
pars pro toto contorted as pool tarp over wood-pile stretched in case it rained
or something worse, what's happened to us with whom so much of what looks
like ought there out Ma's picture window, you on featureless arête I imagine
your lush mantis tops one sego bulb, yours whose trappist face the typicality
of my recognition loaned aptly this queer pentecostal light as that which caught
grandmother's ring she gave me lost in beach rocks' intercostal space, wedged,
her fingers slim, it slipped off these, allotted weft won't pull through clean, desire
projected more than co-substantiates, moodily you camped in doorjamb here
I'd take, you remember yourself, you in ochre wingback, you in thrift-shop folding
chair I would since all good stuff goes as orgasm does, is good and gone that quick,
some recompense: granddaughter of a second wife whose parents were first cousins
farming capers on a cliff open to being glossed, we preambulate, hair in her face,
we walk the walk before the walk not steady down collector roads, you're fitful
at defunct silo, steel hoop-compressed, of grain or something I don't know, pressure
of his static increasing as it goes against precast concrete staves that intermesh,
in tea dress unstiff from steel stays we wove in blueberry field, the field not burnt
this year for cultivation, next, my dress stained from the field we left among
our managed native stands of lowbrush wild fruit magnetic tape and memory card
as well, I guess, we're neither, we're neither, we're both, pretty to think, not steady
down collector road's trim shoulder, hair in her face, nowhere highbrush cultivars.

#5

Then I was a fifth-grade Ophelia, unkempt, or light as a feather, stiff
as a board, was prone on the hood of your serviceable car, mare-like
stalled, were recondite and shifting shrubs usually erect prostrate
about her bioload, sand in our culverts here, as if it neatly added up
after winter, come fill this more out with ideas of causeway, the surf,
one contrail with another mingled, two in sky disperse, too congenitally
inept to consummate a thing who burns up the slash pile—brush, excess,
dead pets—biennially and walks his property line and marks it off
packs down a filial trail subtly through several deer yards there. "Yes,
well I imagined other settings for our unease than this," John said of her
aunt's in Providence we visited and tanks of cranberries where she lived
was borderline before was passed that trait down noticeably to strawberry
blondes, most quiet ones, first cousins before both bogs were drained.
You loved your pallid lace and neon nighties would melt on you should fire
break so you won't wear. You love your pallid nighties, not your extended
terms of credit, therefore only what I'll use I'll haul you under awning,
arborlike, half viewable from dock, a nonpoint source in plum maillot
she doubles back and frets upon and cancels local impish gorse out,
gaff in her head act, I. "Now I'm mortified," John said. Bioavailable
in begonia bed, fat toad my sister landed in, barn snake parts jumping
still, chickens by their necks grandmother swung, church clothes still on,
I'm mortified, don't have the nerve, won't play boldly against my type
more beautiful than myself, our central fact, a new sentence is a sentence
between two sentences, how religion is, knowing what to practice that day,

as if it neatly added up, didn't clog the drains, didn't flood that way
or logging road, as if your engine weren't flooded, as if they hadn't
drained both bogs but flooded these for harvest, corralled by floating
booms—you and I and she—and shook from vine by water reel,
advanced to release another. Begonia bed on second thought not paved
over clean, lawn extruded through some middle, seduced through several
stages of grief, through nodal limbo Heparinized, injections of it daily
in my middle, prone on the hood of his serviceable car, whatever's
in a contrail makes us see what passed before, maybe moments ago,
hours maybe, depends on wind: Wasn't right me dragging her around
like that, wasn't me dragging her around.

Then I was a fifth-grade Ophelia, suspect, new wave, night sweat, inside
thick halo of mouchettes seemed largely to exist at legal tender age, tangles
your impossible form as click world pictures by, a new wave the effect
it caused self-corrects your random sandbar shoreward or stern river
builds sufficient head and breaks clear through bog laurel put on earth
this little space my desire for desire forms, I'm saying, making substitutions,
things they wouldn't talk about but I could tell in babyhood was something
going on like singing along briefly it encounters Vivian Girls, Red Rose Girls,
packs of girls marauding, sisters plural and so sexless—social, lissome, tenseless—
disappear behind a single line. That being done unloaded quantities
of gravel, spread it, raked it out on sandbar lunched on peaches. Later
in rare way happy to see Muriel repair taciturn to my sun parlor, comorbid
expectations, only so much heaven on the screen it looks to me as though
what this calls for is establishment of losses, all the cake in the world, a sort
of prettiness nonetheless, nothing like how Mark's road we came in on bent, copied,
disc mayweed copied along it, weed copied around your press pool clear no
sooner full than begins sward here to thin more than her frame she drowsed on,
floral scarf balled in her hand he clutched, what we thought an heirloom was,
mortal shakes, stains, those cigarettes you wasted, "fog comes on little cat feet,"
said Carl said my grandmother. Grass widow of a Boston marriage left
in Reaganville, couldn't leave, cried. She said, "They are happy," they aren't
anything these boys I think who take, who could, each other's arm in morning
stuff this usual and do this thing together slowly on come morning when
of a sudden trees begin to thin and sward, was older then, that hump that

if you hit it going 55 will flip your stomach Dad would always rev before
tall addled horses from abuse gnaw grooves in fence on River Road from things
we didn't talk about, don't press, not at the dinner table here, not our Cold War
era altar boy, would ask you further questions of the self's own act, of Ruby Ridge,
would conscientiously object, coaxed out rounds toward where things dear
are revenant, not reproduced in whole or part of Lysette's heart spills
well the little totals, this in the wrong hands, actions in the field we'll never,
affairs not recommended: "Be reasonable," she said. "Seems fairly stock,"
better to say. You far off there not fair enough, I want my actual whim,
if circadian should quit him definitely, the mystery, the folding of clothes,
peaches you stole when already you'd stored away peaches after all he'd
done the strangest things we didn't talk about, warm for the very first
every in the party poured out and licked his ice cream cone, poured
out and clucked, "Sous les pavés, la plage? No, under the pavestones,
the beach." Really now to know or have it featured is within bog laurel
where entire margins revolute, within mere halo of mouchettes, when older
palm wine in the head, one doeling mid my phlox ablaze or wild turkey flock
optically was real, was happy, wasn't anything at all, in Vietnam
Dad said they aren't boys just morning stuff this usual. Couldn't leave,
we tried, for cooler greener hill stations iff for prospect poetry.

Clutched in the hot hand / of the child, the flowers
wilt / before we get home.   —Paul Goodman

GAP GARDENING II

If we don't garden the tongue, / they'll blacktop it over.   —Gerry Gilbert

Vermilion border

Person, songer, who trembles,
crossing, to appear what is
belong, I get what is like caught
in spectacular cut or rill of afternoon
you sucked it hours complacent
as barn swallow before white sky
turned blue, of course, don't know
what to do about, have this beloved
problem now, complex, sward-thick
of referents, tumbles, tactically
loosens up, I hope, water kept
on too long softens it, makes subject
us to coarser grass, appealingly
annulled in Emily's hour of lead
"where five cows lay in sun
in droves black swine wandered
unchecked a brown forest stream
swirled down the center of this,"
Arthur almost said. "Outlandish
micro-friction," she said, in vino,
of bimodal life, strong wind.
Scratches only the surface, only
reorganizes the labor, projected
onto undulant field you spread
inviolate her yellow coat out on
for Arthur in white raiment, very.
Fewer deer beds here than years
before, no runoff drainage, coarser grass.

Refugium compendium

For want for wheel-rut, limpet dear, after precious absence lent, post lumpish eden, was dicey, this route you took, in all its faddle, othered. Damn you! For down your bridle path we went, not hand in hand, not coted, faded, see, once lovers in some other life not now in hours spent, strived for, or as you do impute, heels nearish stove, crying, "Whereat, wheatear?" whereupon dawn came as you never did all those years, those hours not ours, limbic, out of reach, and on and on, and dawn came as we, dicey, hissing, lumpish, strode for want the rut so able in our loiter, delicate, as that logjam we waited on as children, articulate, in that vernal stream to break apart and go; was changeable this life for that, these hours for those, some commedia of it on this bridle path, not rushing past, sad perhaps, but only drool, who would not go and disembark, who would only ever age. Look, the wheatear and her rival lark sweet cantillate what we cannot on this, this noon of murk, and in their warble wimble murk increasingly. Say, for want for foolish well-made coition—quantum, limpid, othering: it—but this all is what is none but beseeching makes it so so we stroll not hand in hand along the beeches tall whereat the vatic wheatear fusses and she sings.

Paradox of heap, circa 1943

Drowsy leant against this tallish counterscarp we dug,
sodden now, foundered in the grass, only sour milk
to drink and tack, lids three-quarters closed, one thin
garter I behold, lace teal, I've never seen nor her rare form
rubbed anise oil soft through Persian blinds unclasping
fussy straps, shoes she's quick to leave behind to go off
traipsing toward that sassafras, upon this gainly leans,
swats at flies while here so far away I squat in— Let's depart
next time we do as fools from mud who've been blithely
rolling in it, sluggish, from each other, cassocks off, so warm,
so heavy with the stuff and stained as dahlia tubers are
she's pulling up in knots I wish she'd put down soon to tend
to bind me to this spot and not the beachhead of their stour
since left behind one hour still I glimpse some shred, a weed,
looks at this angle slack from beak as would loose around
her ankle; even rings in rankly water of our trench shook as
troops pass might be a late report of her penny in Ma's vase
to keep those ochre dahlias' pretty petals fresher longer.

Ode of the stirrer-up-of

Here where spring's first pair last leapt
primed berries, purple, bleed; are wet
as what melts on my wrist you hold
to cool me down against this dray
propped at our knoll, gold-brown,
though, see, uncoupled, we, of course,
as she of prolix eros, fair, is so roe-swollen
now, not coaxial with Herring Cove
nor my little articulate cairn we built
nearby your father's horse farm, horseless
now, all mud and forb grown thick
within his concrete well-curb, fern-blurred.
There where those two roads end looks
they've left some tools out in the rain
and in a cleft of rock my box of paints.

By industrial tools I mean all the tools that cannot be produced by one man, as for instance the S.S. Queen Mary. With this definition, we find that the spoken word, which took a minimum of two humans to develop, was the first industrial tool. It brought about the progressive integration of all individual generation-to-generation experiences and thoughts of all humanity everywhere and everywhen. The Bible says, "In the beginning was the word"; I say to you, "In the beginning of industrialization was the spoken word."

—R. Buckminster Fuller

Song of a superfund site

Of redly murky dielectric trough
and soughing pines I sing at rim
of gravel pit on which snow sick
in general falls oblique, loads down
these yellow flags, invasive sieves,
on which she backslid, combed into
the zone where I belong or would
by his initial parallax, her pink
taut face ill-matched with single
instant of release when one heel
snagged a branch aside my sump,
she thrust or slipped amid those shafts
and shifting stalks or husks dried up
from opaque needle ice. But there
they go again to shake it off along
that split silt fence much like our
thrown seine net as if this was my
want of who he was to me ago.

Quaquaversal

In anteroom, on riverboat—my vox
in clammy anteroom, deserted: Were
inert as auks in warmer wastes, was how
we leaned, were made more lost, now not
so brave as we might want, perplexed,
more vexed, by banks of Yangtze River
thrumming, unmoved, while she shivered,
huddled under cloth. Was wet, was cool,
was bright; her shoulders brown; were brown
from all the sauntering we did that day about
his gorge, that small one there, was round,
she fraught and leaning on this onyx still
obstreperous and taut, plus sauntered on,
three more days gone, just prattled on,
just safflower picked, contriving sicko songs
while ready ever one ear to these waters,
strong, for thuds of poles dropped in by men,
them old, to move their boats along, those same,
you see, we longed to eddy down this river
on, yet never did, not ever, all my fault,
three ways gone wrong. Least thought to dip
the cloth, hers white, so pale as great auk's
paunch, which skimmed this quarry freshet,
blessed, or of it what was left, was mostly dry,

forgot, to drape her, soothe her neck, to make
her bear some mantle where was radiant, so blithe,
to let me think I could a vision, one, though,
shivered by the river as I balked. Oh, say out
at droughted freshet how it's not my turn
to want this; then would not know now
was my turn then to step into that freshet.

Paradox of heap, circa 1945

Suppose at slatternly hepatica in haughty lampen light
or in rushes sounds of seducing Cynthia on rusty winches
were one sound while surplus Ural girls in moon-silk
robes coax flim fleurs from this road beyond that impasse
where some adder suns itself just as you do with civvies
off within palmetto leaves, bundle these in brickle jar,
spare water glass, milk bottle emptied of the last to sell
to buy more stocking paint and pout or rut in view
of lapwings which the double-dream slow sifted down
spadefuls' outflow of char for at their sandbar, we
deux contemplate our paradox of heap and tell us
lies, hushed that she'd only sleep the way we all did
once at those now burnt out Sutro Baths.

Superior mirage

When air below the line of sight
is cooler than above then was
pigeon-toed, was carrot-topped,
my love whose Coke can rolled
the span of her long tarmac drive
where a cat coughed up the mouse
below my bougainvillea our host
whole totters out of, droll, his head
cinched with scotoma, sees one
fata morgana, some coleoptera
carom off queen carobs in suspension.
Later on goes something like: Glum,
slumped low, still drunk, in Ma's white
clawfoot, wet, he gazed hard into
distance off, raglimp, as was the scene,
moth-brown from your mud-sore feet,
bath sloshed on thick-slat floor I blind
nailed down. So nice to feel not like
one must do a thing when from
your winch house was so moved
to watch land-locked salmon move
I remember where the bunchgrass balds
below two alder shrubs more adders visit
on occasion, mate beside perhaps, coiled
up much dried thick moult like littered
cellophane. Over his mouth of her body.

Rough for

What a rare bird you are in your yearning for a town formed by shore only, for summer love, for everything in triplicate, for the strength to survive even his Delphic, even quietly while it spasms, disappears, but possesses too or doesn't disappear at all, as they say, but we know how it goes, that we are strange, out of luck, demanding, and what a rare bird are you, your letting go of and coming back superimposed, grafted to a patch of dusty earth, foolhardy in resilience, ours, who caught each other one by one necking in the hall, each the other caught and turned into rare bird before this ground we walk, lingers, shuffles, shoves in the pear and cake meantime no one let her in, our mouths were full we said, all apologies, but wouldn't it not do to— but you flew always to the spear-point of things, pinned often roses on the each of us, inebriated, each of us, at the time in some way, in one way or a fist in the mouth and not pear not wine not cake, and still it wouldn't do so you'd go on screaming like that on some corner on some street, maybe Delphic in some way, drifting into reverie among snow drifts grayed away with— while her furniture was pawned off piece by piece you placed each rare bird on a point with this means that and so on ran in all directions with dirty glasses on and came to, possessing still, not stopping up her giggles as she should, would not do well inevitably, vanished at the last, vigorously, whole, into a drum, dreaming rose gardens and birthday cake, Sinatra and flat-heeled shoes, the oracle come to, of Hong Kong and the nuns panting on Grand, not letting you in, you letting go, whole and— and in the end, foolhardy, yes, as little foxes among wax lilies who feed in row and after row but my own row I've not kept as you can see with your dove's eyes, I've not, even with this banner overhead of love, even with our love cipher safe in some rock cleft, or in pieces and in several clefts, or she only a pillar of smoke moving out from wilderness but one they sing to and fetch for.

Flying around, these birds gradually discovered that there were certain places in which that particular marine life tended to pocket—in the marshes along certain ocean shores of certain lands. So, instead of flying aimlessly for chance finding of that marine life they went to where it was concentrated in bayside marshes. After a while, the water began to recede in the marshes, because the earth's polar ice cap was beginning to increase. Only the birds with very long beaks could reach deeply enough in the marsh holes to get at the marine life. The unfed, short-billed birds died off. This left only the long-beakers. When the birds' inborn drive to reproduce occurred there were only other long-beakers surviving with whom to breed. This concentrated their long-beak genes. So, with continually receding waters and generation to generation inbreeding, longer and longer beaked birds were produced. The waters kept receding, and the beaks of successive generations of the birds grew bigger and bigger. The long-beakers seemed to be prospering when all at once there was a great fire in the marshes. It was discovered that because their beaks had become so heavy these birds could no longer fly. They could not escape the flames by flying out of the marsh. Waddling on their legs they were too slow to escape, and so they perished. This is typical of the way in which extinction occurs—through over-specialization.

—R. Buckminster Fuller

Long shore drift

for Katherine Craig, who drew beautiful pictures (1986-2007)

Dawn in bawdy columns comes,
preempts your illdyed object's tread
steep up four baize-lined feeder bluffs
divided parallely, rife with basal moss
or uncollated river scrub unclear
just what his use is of a rose deinterlaced
from crop-stalk waste she writhed in,
overlooking, extradiagetic, nothing
as remembered where those splintered
pierstakes were that interpenetrate
tidewrack and mud we'd swum among,
pushed off by serial transmission
summed my wild stippled tit consumingly
for whom this winter ranges yet
was not my Kate whose prefab death
at dawn bowed hoary boughs out back
below faux plenilune, your object's hem
a little lifted with low ozone iff
she swung, her cited causal qualia fled
this way I quiet plod their pier
to boldly suck one viscid subdivided
somaclonal orange wedge.

No possible relations between an actor and a tree.
The two belong to different worlds. (A stage tree
simulates a real tree.) —Robert Bresson

She admitted to finding less time lately for doing: going to an aikido class, cooking a meal, phoning the children, maintaining love affairs. But for wondering there seemed all the time in the world—hours, whole days. Wondering? "About..." she said, looking at the ground. "Oh, I might start wondering about the relation of that leaf"—pointing to one—"to that one," pointing to a neighbor leaf, also yellowing, its frayed tip almost perpendicular to the first

THE HAWK VISIT

one's spine. "Why are they lying there just like that? Why not some other way?" "I'll play: 'Cause that's how they fell down from the tree." "But there's a relation. A connection..." Julia, sister, poor moneyed waif, you're crazy. (A crazy question: one that shouldn't be asked.) But I didn't say that. I said: "You shouldn't ask yourself questions you can't answer." No reply. "Even if you could answer a question like that, you wouldn't know you had." —Susan Sontag

I set out to write a poem, to write some thing, for your birthday, Robert—and each try it ended up a love poem for Ruth—shared distance of love you would knowing say—persistent longing of a life—no glittering of just one leaf on the cottonwood but all glitter, till just one leaf—and do not the last few always go at once, together?
—Kenneth Irby

to the prolapsarian

I.

Where the land begins, a stunted trunk, like that one new-grown in Sassetta, bearing
one leaf only and only one persimmon; where the women begin but see wine on their
mouths and then won't say anything, not each of the other's stain, of her stain, and hers
and hers. There a swain's hawk low swoops looking for a rat where you two visit in the
grass and shimmy down, looking down your noses at— but I'm where is the magnolia-
white shade, are the green slippers, ribbon-laced and flat-heeled; where are the twelve
yards even of skirt and sunburnt hands folded in some lap; is a bantam face, drowsy,
twitching in the shade; where the animals are too big for a hawk's getting. They wave
their wide-brimmed Panama hats at— but I'm where is the split-rail fence, the soft field,
squiring lightly and idling in that sun come through my mint-garnished glass, demure;
me demure in tight-fitting basque, hands folded, still...

II.

Plain and tame in constitution you move to set my cap for that sly piece in oak grove politicking, or in sumac, rather, in many ways not at all remarkable, no, in gory sun, half-hearted, two-faced, still meaning well, and deep of dimple, spare of waist, who fidgets, gabbles, goes on unable to endure any man in love with any woman not her. Damned gory sun, damned earth turned over and over and furrows curved such that what will won't now wash away but too that I won't find my footing here, where it all is vapors and lemon verbena, all is bright and blank and scared. Still, there were younger yet than she than I yet she was fine then as she was no matter not so much as now as fullest poppy fallen, as lapsed eve, as yellow salicaire fallen in saltire, as italicked split-rail through which you pass and Eden passed and the Ennead birdwatched by, the birds stirred from austere. They did this fussy, too ready to flap and squawk at slightest move while where you were you rubbed verbena on your skin and on his and bit his and sucked some venom out and spat it out of some snake in grass. See, they sensed this and flapped and fussed not guessing where they were, the birds, that this memoria might come pose some threat, might warp all dreamed variants of our much-loved such-and-such a place. That is, what might happen to you on dreaming of this? On rebutting? On swallowing it? Where it falls from the sky of all things.

III.

Or else as the clinamen of sweet cyclamen, how each swerves to come loose—one petal laid upon your face, then two petals: bewitching the bantams they both.

IV.

At coppice precipice, the celestial stretto set, with factness his pervasive ongoingness sheers off, or with pervasive factness does this do this: bears itself as bantling portage beneath that ochre arch of Sharon where she lay the flowers down—the rose, next noble yarrow, her yellow salicaire—where they still patter sing and caterwaul of him and us, however many of us. Yet this all has yet to do with how it happened that he sheered off, inter alia, he who when at dusk would turn over it speechless, glowered, who took what I took from me, who disordered apostrophe of—oh, dulcet null set!—who inventoried anathema for us gorgeously, so generous, he, but the hawk, see, and not the man who shimmied down. But I'm where is the man see.

V.

Mariana in the mowed-down green or years on in outmoded range, punch drunk and without a lover, in illo ordine, thought saw near-stars illimited, thought heard frog's song out back below the lower forty of wheat or peat grass or somesuch; thought who might go down on her in Coventry had gone for good and her womb lapsed in eve, the both shoved out, not young, and now who is young is left—heaven forfend!—or else likened to witchy imposture gone off into some wrong idea and now knee-deep in it, indecorous (but by friar's lantern found shepherd's purse to staunch it).

Am made a fool or made a fool for this, that we in ways do standardly dream would have something there at the end, in some set of ways, in ways more than none—hark the over-soul! But too doubt dearth of vox in clammy anterooms, deserted; doubt would strike pay dirt in preface to one's soft maternal ditch and sung that long haul of preface throughout this merry metropicalis while we leery on hiatus redounded and knocked against each other; each sung moony incomparable arbituaries to whom effortless inventory anathema, who depose thigh, spot hawk in sky, whose sky view is askew, numinous, rare, but in a voice, sung, even we not of it love.

It would not have been long since slipperied I'd rolled, lame; this was since then I did not know really what I was talking. And yet clearer it becomes: Mariana in delirium sine fine—so much depends on this.

VI.

Frozen trees one by one one after the into Canyon fall; you called me your lover then, or willing, only willing. And too was she? And who was he? Only your little eanlings then who mewled for who far-flew that coppice precipice.

VII.

Already I've promised all my dances away, not young, where pink froth flanks the new-turned clay; but you saw only one hawk that day, you two, so long ago, and made me to attend. That, and a tree, a split trunk, mimicking the orders of my earlier mind—back and forth— So I'll think of this as the hawk visit, no matter the porch, the fence, no matter my sitting here so well, so long, so far from... all these hours sitting here. Once we shared a common city, looking always for that same hawk, and well-taught, we, in what this meant. Later was your wife first proffered forth the bird... But look, this inscrutable sarabande now seems— or, say, our so-called dreamer that day at the World's Fair, going where he might best unforget it—this inscrutable, a parable, that recent world: him, for whom eros was everything, a stream tugging between two posts, one thrush on my thresh in eve, was what I broke my compass on and my compass. See, the longer I stay in any one place, the clearer it becomes: Where the land begins, she does—so ill at ease, and apparency thus folioed, and fallen from the sky, and gone off at an angle.

VIII.

So are we still only suffixes of hawk? Will this suffice the one mind for want of a thousand hand? At holy-lonely precipice these are questions that come up. What remains to be done.

And I won't tell you where it is, so why do I tell you / anything?
Because you still listen, because in times like these / to have you
listen at all, it's necessary / to talk about trees.   —Adrienne Rich

FROM A GRAFTED TREE

Follow your own femoral artery long enough you'll find it
leads you into the body of another person. This kind of love
the ancients called The Fine Red Thinking.   —Robert Kelly

...I too am a rare / Pattern. As I wander
down / The garden paths...   —Amy Lowell

Future tires building herds

on quitting that day job

Where late in future pasture
one day summer selects
something like a family
on this clothesline also waits
familiar handsome student
midst what grows in tires left
grows as blanched-out sticks
revive, thanks especial golden
finchness owed Elizabeth
quenches time enough to earn
her keep. That red dumb wine,
bring it, your rural dream
midday working in my building
perks up Willis, votes to live
a little better or fail new era
of good feeling for this clean
well-lighted place as Jen's
unequal gray of doe is
unequally gentle in herds.

For platonic loves your perfect form

Returns offseason John's sot-weed
you blur and feed-lot grass, your face
in John's like waking up supernally
a summer essay, no root, like raking
it up in dozens offhand the glamour of
John's normal song moments under
klieg lights washed up only that best
part of Seine waves at this she coaxes.

Unreasonable pastoral

That cyclically real obstacle the warm,
heavy, instant heart June samples
wingéd over sorghum fields entirely
a floodway series, always wild, female
imagination not civic pride fat-oiled
my frog rumored cries for Edna,
children gone missing this season
someone sprayed for like this film
interrupts itself practically you might
trace when feeling cultish by red
thread iff necessary, intolerates
material fact weakly, heavy breathing,
branch-crotch Zoë talks about
the yard, our crop loss, getting old.

Riparian buffer zone song for deep vein thrombosis

Things I loved were having a body
this loped, armful of warm girl, fat rain,
sweet relief, fat fruit. My fatigue is found

like fruit some fugal gladness wets, hears
nothing at all, no system preferred as if
the sun won't wound it must be gold

and greenly veined beside your longing,
your leg hanging over lip of low-dose
light or Chris's near shore you review

she leans against a certain way unperfectly
to occupy Claire's "screaming little car,"
these little losses by addition even noxious

milfoil in loops, loops looped, blended
from looping, a working back from
what I do not love, a pond upon a pond

dotes our pond, our spillage parts
with sameness there, part Gustave's
pinnate leaves more sentences dissimulate.

Wolf-songbird complex

Hooverville, Reaganville, Bloombergville, et al.

Into restless profusion core figure must as Mina "spring from stepping stone
to stone" in fallow land in your blue shirt there came to be a set of things made

contact with like lavender border her curtilage grown becomes whole bank of lavender
what only was a border knows intimately, licking out fine balance. What is it to say to want

to live some place else and not, some way else and not? Among others you are accumulation
—air miles, minutes, traces, dust passion perfects the form world indebted to us

willed. Count this, all will come down to this, this as you count lavender from hard chair
a level unexpected but do not borrow against since it's getting colder now, moved rapidly by

description through bipartisan grief in bonus army surplus, sweet poster child, agony aunt.
Paul's lust is loyal, leads him out, Robert's desire practically radical, goes beyond our curtilage

so black one bluff with weather it stretches me apart from lyric a songbird some wolf he claims
to be alone mine, my forms, my meanings, however many is many "timid people,

black with despair" have "lost faith in the American system"? Save from our fold
of foil enough last traces of butter; remember Grandma Eleanor in that era always did.

Four lives mixed up, a loess poiesis

> with Ted Dodson, Ben Fama, Dylan Thomas,
> William Ernest Henley, et al.

On spit shoals mussel-pooled, blue heron-priested peeks from sharp hat for the most
part wasted, tight in bra your mother'd bought me suns were never hot then, draped

across hot rumble seat pivotally spoils our afternoon but a name over and over is nice
arms around it really, there is no practice wild but Edna's practice crisp air features

when not leaving others wanting every thing they saw once folded with wet picture
dreamed woke standing in she's meaning miles away: Edna, Zelda, Melanctha all along

dirt road one always wore that yellow coat, green hat, one always took one off, grievable
even, brackish night covers me a pit from pole to pole you won't believe such forms

it takes by any means the very last so live right now more possibly as you can search out
gold, rework washings, wold waste piles, work your mouth on a dish, arugula bunches

my weight wants to fall upon equally could run something over as pretty, abject, mixed in soil
surface management brings me single solid appearance: get up, little girl, for this is loess

poiesis, lost amid long list false city's wildflowers afloat with plans entirely new was eminent
domain our trashy world, no, curtilage entirely and radio plays central to night, Nina Simone.

September in situ

Red fox gull-swooped frames
lawn cypress extra meanings
glimmer, dead zone or not
your claims are not my lord,
I am not eloquent, typical
source grows virtue-like a spell
Eros models all we know slips,
hurries to say shop aisle is dark
ride, sea stud, slips force of
revelation vast middle portions
naturally little have considered
more inestimable the park—
airfield, woodlot—greater
the implications of her vogue
solicitude pretend you are
prolific breed, resembles Schiele
girl in green most central cypress,
losses by addition even salient,
nonporous—rock garden rock,
pool tile, patio brick. "I run
to the rock, please hide me...
The rock cried out, 'I can't hide you.'"

Truly migratory

> "Come from always, you will go away everywhere." —Arthur Rimbaud
> "Come/as you are/as you were/as I want you to be." —Kurt Cobain

Things you say in the moment as iff
they're things to say in the moment you've
been thinking about for years, try
to think a figure for this, watershed

in a cold snap, surface something
to look at, stroke the farthest from
direct supply, deposits going soft
upon surf zone, foam, spit

of land disappears in miles pink
in sequence erupts first place my body
rejects far reach wind-handled fills
orders about her head stars shade

to public quality walking in
tall spikerush boyish chorus fells
before cell tower, lanky lovers
on brown river on black inner

tube, the backwash, ankle socks,
fish ladder boys drowned against,
crickets, getting over: We don't
develop adequate image

stars refuse to privately hold.

Universe is an evolutionary-process scenario without beginning or end, because the shown part is continually transformed chemically into fresh film and reexposed to the ever self-reorganizing process of latest thought realizations which must continually introduce new significance into the freshly written description of the ever-transforming events before splicing the film in again for its next projection phase.

—R. Buckminster Fuller

Sodus II

for Yinfei Wu

Assorodus, demure for once
you xerox me a starry night
damp flowers path, the monocrop
bee-quiet evolves matutinal song
of agony aunt heart-fracking until
cold planets, ticking, cease, Amanda
says, difference island to island
delights this useful little book
when she feels alien, why
the lady is a tramp, develops
materrateral song from Alexander's
hand immaculate and chaste
sower of the waste into
grooves my arm around my waist.

Turning on an erotic theme

Merrily casual our city floats, a catheter
lifting sluggish mists, defrosts skylight
lower branches trim, satisfies his torture

to be a thought on landscape disfigured
tediously through abbreviation, asks "you"
from cupola popular but heat-sick "come"

along dark mountains tremulous with
companionship, fizzy air, little story I
dedicate, paper wine, alcohol water, Ted's

thin ocean juice, vernal beer your balmy
sport or normal saline till finally no field, no
time to pin hair straight, anyway she leaves

before the wedding, like school, not enough
dresses, special sleep among some relatives
daily wadded up for languor, network

television, Ada on the railing has a boyfriend
surly with championship. What a breeze
achieves in tangles scoops my skirt, hers

you fix as covers after, live oaks list, it's trying
to mean we stumble, idiot heart again
healed through abbreviation, day becomes

very different, foggy trip, an inch more
air, couldn't have been hopeful: beautiful
room so full, this is so few of my books.

It's geworfenheit

for Randy Lee Maitland

Haunted by the public part
jars make dark a sycamore
type with wine, coquette shapes
untrifled no one buttoned up
soft as from small drug such bark
in plates improves my mind,
geraniums again the cutting
garden stores she slept like after
swimming or low roof light bent
above, you thought we were
boys without forests, hedgerows
hardly hedgerows, figures, little
lines thrown native to her
throwing in some part
of dark cubic acres song
it is hard to say I feel bad for it
knows climate change will come,
our finest single forms fund
this clearing, this accurately—
there's lace where it's unbuttoned,
torn, canvas, grass, there's nothing
like a retaining wall.

Its surface effect on Mary, John, Melanctha, Jeff

We were strong to love this store
was very heaven wanting to stay
so leaving is a dreary car or
constitutes your dreary car
performance, dumbs all talk
of ripe of both, old growth

and tender crop the same
unbuttons the man you are in
some dark aisle smally adjusts
after warbles our steering a tweet
he'll probably regret the same
room as her cousin, we were

strong not going anywhere in
my Honda always wine-soft always
taking home the terror object, only
so much grocery etiquette permits
deep cuts to old growth since
green ideas sleep furiously when

staunch half-gods go our screen
doors slam since Mary's dress
waves by example toward
adjacent just-cleared lot since it's
unbuttoned I was led to take
an eager part in clearing.

Poet's work

for Claire Devoogd & Claire Donato

Here starry Mary's made
of something you might want,
went toward real trees if that's
feeling required, really he tried
to remember the job, division
leaps, affection spent setless
as a spill how we all wish to go
home together this many dreams
removed herds another over
heart, loose card of light enough
repressed thrill perfectly expressed
in switches in crabgrass heard
through original door cider spills
down he threw, started upstate, you
must picture of me delight, single
new study though not spectacular
local blossoms all of right now
collected for me to like very much.

Leisure arts sisters brothers

with Jennifer Nelson & Andrew Durbin

Certain of my emergencies the personality
of modern catastrophe, pylons into earth
grusomely cut, grass too much cleared
away from benches, some cannery glowing
up, incredibly gaining, the crackle, it's
a mark of you alone, so look at sex
and think of nothing, sea splashings,
rowlocks' clunk, sunny waste sunk below
her line flashes out prized this noon
like that you went with civic thump
heals proof over stylish, dirigible flusher,
twists, curls in yellow short shorts or
in the quality of short shorts, how you went
our little garden stretches me to him.

Sweet mother

for Corina Copp

Her kindness always ahead of us
John posed quiet someone feelingly
known to be small, lunched, remember
let's ask the dietician about, pink

pullable clothes, delicate hubbub
ee stood thinking anything, morning,
enormous room, maybe the world
—reed bed, row cover, backlot. It's

therblig vs. glad hand, your guns
vs. butter. She sups on whatever
like Joni I could drink a case of slowly
gossips, who cares if I stay standing

who cares for affective memory
anymore if animals might go around
polite in daytime backlot and I've
a ribbon to hide my hair.

Million bell

Gunmetal million bell
this wide of the mark
tip cuttings propagate

like seaside tickets go
to his sweetheart with
hot little breath for sea

lion woman on medicine
lake, makes quick work,
sends broth up, post-

sentiment remotely studies
without dreary interpretation
sublime interruption, how

easily sucked in, both fish,
my dreams I bought I'll
drown my book, clean sack

of sun, it's only natural, world,
as far as your desires go you
seem pretty real if modular.

Gut flora

Phlox in a jar softens from
the sphere of it, the whole
sagging thing too distracted
to be very kind which is weary
you hurry my Cori not wrong
about this prayerly in shapewear
cut through here for bringing
a case, you again tipsy told
her I was nice, very mobilized
with hotter eyes all at the top
bottles little assaults on safety,
bald baby in her backseat gums
pink pastry, witchy necessary
habits flower his chest how Sharon's
secular crepuscular sky gathers
to its sky indescribability then
longish in learned airlock entry
together imagine to be rubbed
clear everywhere like cleanser.

Active system

Ran through car lots like belonged
flossy substitute from the start
not to understand just kissing
more than open shirts, snakes
over turf, hyperaccumulators, roots
that propagate laterally desirable
for tees, fairways, soft as chalk, kissing
him apart to adequate information
—what's a fairway anyway? Reedy
roadbed, inadequate aqueduct, heavy
metals poured on this which sucks up
heavy metals. Enjoy your formal phasms,
squeeze my hand hard as it hurts or fly
up with them in a network, revival field.

Jeff's undergarment meadow near a permabank

Control release transparent song   ·
in wavers, flash, like pleasure leaks

meadow-still less slip strap slips
who's learned to tell the difference, this

first sound of our night crowd, Lisa's
learned to speak expensively to

my passive amassment amazement to
your credit, sober dreamy station.

Flyover country

for Jamie Barret Riley & Hannah Hancock Rubinsky

Was only smoke held up
his dress, will go for spangles

at edge of the world, whiskey
pine, long song, just a flat

black form in paper wind, rag
of ragtop and night together

rolled up you must shine
on in patterns like flight patterns.

Think of it. We are blessed with technology that would be indescribable to our forefathers. We have the wherewithal, the know-it-all to feed everybody, clothe everybody, and give every human on earth a chance. We know now what we could never have known before—that we now have the option for all humanity to make it successfully on this planet in this lifetime. Whether it is to be Utopia or Oblivion will be a touch-and-go relay race right up to the final moment.

—R. Buckminster Fuller

Love letter to my detriment

Dear adhocrat whose fresh pressure disgorges from creatures of statute infernal
treacle while smokes wait over breasts sunk into our cottage (deeper than a pattern
in its china) where plushy election requires true blush of petition please refresh my feeble dress
more capable of rippling so invisible the work to stimulate experience as commitment, oh
rebarbative hosiery I don not to break with that aroma of diacritical fellowship in vegetal
years spent acring around blustery Amerarcana vale in calyceal repubescence, winds persuasive
by collection admitted to cafés downstairs, each calibrative bushel, all sugar bears, administers
bicameral remembrance toward considerable frugality and frugality extinguished, toward every
day we are repatriated more and more into the sun says Dana and whatever, toward what
we'd do extinguishing monstrous debt since sentimental education and otherwise regular
harmless hours, lyrical shruggery, unruly sexual lives with gritty lovers and considerably
fragile lovers, votive lovers, who wouldn't leave that tiny house, meanwhile toward chaotic
appeal the ornamental grasses smartly she swoons in, her disheveled model's feat, and this
capricious business of instinctive worship for power and for the famously deskilled, are my worries
so inscrutable, toward trusty phalanx warmed in soft clothes on rocks inscribing ocean I had
swum, its entire articulation, and regular useless kids having everything, meaning nothing, he's
drunk again, toward imagining tiny houses and building tiny houses in their yard, fed Bianca's
guerilla cart into massive mottled wood perfecting loyal encounter with collective cake
my clumsy hands split all your wonderful hair toward, toward vague coffees downstairs, plural
complaints, little shapes calculated across a spongy map roots correctly quilt even as everywhere
in heaps are the oldest trees and children writing this only hurts, doesn't it, how can we keep
doing already, in my beloved yard, relics, slabs, original flavors' constitutive song, buzz
no drones whereas in some tribal yards are drones, how can we stoke this flare system, toward
discovery in dollops of spontaneous suffrage the future poet grows a variety of bean distilled

from our roughage and Anne's simple mourning speech, I'll find you the recordings. Dear
fragile bureaucrat whose stylish innocence, whose artisanal ethics the mad farmer, lonely
painter squelch, try, like snowmelts at the crux of metals, reveal your aerial show in which
I'm complicit and my friends and our friendship considerably, grouping on kind state with
mercurial vitamins sucks at the heart, neighbor babies in spring's bright muds go where
the bones are farther apart like parochial valentine cloaked between absolute candles reproduces
insufficient song, feeds on what floats up, munites star wreckage especially Amerarcanaan.

Perfect dreams of careful breaking

Leaves in quarters mottle Lindsay
currently and ladle out as errands

light its equal reach, celebrity fern,
vegetable patch the middle river

downs, notes terminal for a tenderness
steward sleepy, hungry girl so rude

toward pillowy garden in grids in gross
alteration finds we come to live by what

we come by, rural norm this granite
smoothed like tracing paper soaked

a length how local usage details come,
happily cola, impracticable people

blotted out night's selvage a path
burned to heap I've questions about

quiet adjustments for Ari once
will approach the same otherwise

he'd explain wouldn't change at all
smooth object, private devotion was

even in car share alone some
matinee delight or patio delight

possibly you must picture of her
open, passional chain grocer,

daily scene itself as solemn as
for parts refloating fragile ship

intact impossible. Book of flexible
hours, flexible doors' exquisite sills'

relief, but in another country I'm
saying too it's hard coming home.

Proof of concept for floating child

for Soren Miller

White the sky settles mirrored
wave pool almost tautologic
causes waves reasonably large
your lyric thinks itself foams
where return canal input
generates a further wave.

Godard: *We're filming a scene in the subway, where it goes up above ground. [...]*
It isn't written yet. I'll write it tomorrow.

Acknowledgments

Versions of these poems first appeared in *The Brooklyn Review, Conjunctions, Lana Turner, LIT, No, Dear, The Recluse, Sentence, SET, Sugar House Review, Sun's Skeleton, Washington Square, Whiskey & Fox,* and *Word For/Word* and in the Argos Books anthology *Why I Am Not A Painter.* Gap Gardening I and II were released together as a chapbook by These Signals Press.

I am especially grateful for the kindness, care, and tip-top verve deployed by editors and curators Emily Brandt, Macgregor Card, Corina Copp, Alex Cuff, Ray DeJesús, Claire Devoogd, Claire Donato, Andrew Durbin, Jeff T. Johnson, David James Miller, Stephen Motika, Jeffrey Joe Nelson, Jennifer Nelson, Dan Owen, Arlo Quint, and Dan Remein.

I am also deeply indebted to early supporters Tonya Foster and Benjamin Mosse and first readers Curtis Jensen, Randy Lee Maitland, Connie Mae Oliver, and Michelle Dupre. Each offered me the charged-up generosity of vision and art of attention so clear in their own practices.

Without the magic of mentorship from Mary Caponegro, Chiori Miyagawa, Julie Agoos, Ben Lerner, Marjorie Welish, and Anselm Berrigan, surely this collection would not have come to pass. As for Robert Kelly, his words and heart light all my leaves, till just one leaf.

This book is dearly dedicated to my mother/advocate Grace, father/philosopher Peter, sister/true songer Gail, a dozen regular friends of steel (love more hardy for its unkempt varietal), fierce darling for life Willis (who too has lived with these pages over years and apartment floors), plus the next crop of blueberry girls, starting with Anna and Stella.

Finally, thank you to the State of Maine, Annandale-on-Hudson, West Philadelphia, Brooklyn, and Lopez Island, variously my homes, real soils. Additional thanks go to all who weave the silver in a line on which this magpie thrives.

About Gracie Leavitt

Gracie Leavitt was born in Massachusetts in 1985, grew up in Maine in a log cabin her parents built, and has made a home in Brooklyn. She holds a BA in human rights from Bard College and an MFA in poetry from Brooklyn College.

ISBN: 978-1-937658-16-8

Design and typesetting by HR Hegnauer
Text set in Bodoni

Cover: Emma Bee Bernstein, "Self-Portrait in the Red Rose Dress" (2007)
Used by permission of the Estate of Emma Bee Bernstein

The excerpt of Philippe Labro's exchange with Jean-Luc Godard is taken from a 1966
interview for *Le Nouveau Candide.*

All R. Buckminster Fuller quotes are taken from *Operating Manual for Spaceship Earth*
(1969) except for the quote on page 77, taken from *Critical Path* (1981).

Cataloging-in-publication data is available from the Library of Congress

Distributed by University Press of New England
One Court Street
Lebanon, NH 03766
www.upne.com

Nightboat Books
Brooklyn & Callicoon, New York
www.nightboat.org

About Nightboat Books

Nightboat Books, a nonprofit organization, seeks to develop audiences for writers whose work resists convention and transcends boundaries. We publish books rich with poignancy, intelligence, and risk. Please visit nightboat.org to learn more about us and how you can support our future publications.

The following individuals have supported the publication of this book. We thank them for their generosity and commitment to the mission of Nightboat Books:

    Elizabeth Motika
    Benjamin Taylor

In addition, this book has been made possible, in part, by grants from The Fund for Poetry, the National Endowment for the Arts, and the New York State Council on the Arts Literature Program. Support was also provided by a Face Out grant, funded by The Jerome Foundation and administered by The Council of Literary Magazines and Presses.

DATE DUE OCT 3 1 2014

MAR 1 0 2016	
	PRINTED IN U.S.A.